RELIGION
Satan's Philosophy of Truth

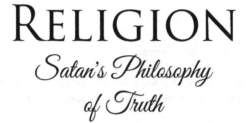

BUBBA

authorHOUSE®

AuthorHouse™
1663 Liberty Drive
Bloomington, IN 47403
www.authorhouse.com
Phone: 1 (800) 839-8640

Published by AuthorHouse 11/30/2016

ISBN: 978-1-5246-5031-5 (sc)
ISBN: 978-1-5246-5030-8 (e)

Library of Congress Control Number: 2016919029

Print information available on the last page.

Scripture quotations marked KJV are from the Holy Bible, King James Version (Authorized Version). First published in 1611. Quoted from the NKJV Classic Reference Bible, Copyright © 1983 by The Zondervan Corporation.

TABLE OF CONTENTS

THIS IS A TRIBUTE OF my gratitude, respect, and admiration for these people and many others not mentioned.

For my lovely wife of twenty-eight years, Vera Gayle Boutwell Traina, I give you my love with gratitude and thanks. For my brother-in-law and sister, Loyd and Mary Jo Nye, I thank you both for your prayers and your understanding of my passion for the Word of God. For my first cousin Gary Joseph Traina, I thank you for understanding my passion as we study scriptures together. I am greatly pleased to see this passion growing in you. Praise God! For my uncle Louis Alphonse Traina, better known to all as Uncle Al, I thank you deeply for your support and your knowledge of my passion as well. As my deceased dad's younger brother, I feel close to him when I am close to you.

For my friends Jamie Gebhart and Felicia Vitrano Banuvong with love as family. Together for the past five years, we have come to a greater knowledge in the Word of God. I am thankful and grateful to have you both in my life. For Beth Majors, a lifelong friend and family member, I thank you for your time and your support.

And last but certainly not least, for He is the beginning and the end of all things, I thank my God in Jesus's name!

Though these people and others may or may not fully agree or understand my views and opinions, we all can agree on one thing: Jesus Christ–Lord, God, and Savior (Isa. 9:6)!

ABOUT THE AUTHOR

I AM A WELDER BY TRADE and a retired member of the boilermakers, local no. 37. I worked for Buck Kreihs company in New Orleans, Louisiana, for most of my welding career. Though I am a licensed hairstylist and a horseshoer, my passion in my skills has always been welding.

Three years of service in the army and a thirty-year welding career has fortunately allowed me to visit many countries. If you have read my first book, My Study, you would know and understand why I claim to be a common man. Though I am not a well-educated man, I do speak with great boldness and authority, pertaining to the Word of God. This is not to say I am an authority of any kind, but a man only with a passion for truth. A man who will stand strong in his opinions and boldly present them to a very opinionated world!

I left the so-called churches of the world over thirty-five years ago. I have read and learned much about the beliefs of many non-Christian religions of the world. I am also knowledgeable about the beliefs of all Christian religions that exist. I do not claim to be a prophet of God or an intellectual. I studied scripture for many years without any denominational doctrine to steer me in understanding of the Word of God. I can boldly say that all, thought of as religions, which are nothing more than organized belief systems of the world, have truth and error. This is why I know, religion can be, and often is, Satan's philosophy of truth. It is not the doctrines of many religions that are important. What matters is knowing Christ Jesus. As children of God, knowing Christ leads us into an intimate relationship as Father and child, as one spirit. We are one in Christ, as Christ is one in the Father. As one Spirit, we are in the family of God and not of this world!

Though I am a common man and a very small figure in a large world, I can clearly see the troubles of the world because of Satan and his philosophy of truth!

INTRODUCTION

THERE IS AN OLD SAYING: "You can lead a horse to water, but you can't make him drink." In the Bible, Jesus speaks of water as the Spirit of everlasting life. He explains this knowledge to the woman at the well (John 4:14). This woman did not understand His Words. She had no clue of the grace that He was offering her. Many of us lack this knowledge as well. To receive it, we must completely digest the Words of Jesus. He is the Spirit of everlasting life.

There is no – religion in the world that can fully give us the nourishment of everlasting life. Look at the very first hint of this truth in the book of Genesis, chapter 3 verse 22: "And the Lord God said, 'Behold, the man has become as one of us, to know good and evil: and now, lest he put forth his hand, and take also of the tree of life, and eat, and live forever'" (NKJV).

If you will notice, the Word of God is speaking of Adam and Eve after they disobeyed Him. This also includes their offspring and the many who would follow thereafter. This, of course, would be known as humankind. If we willingly receive the Words of Jesus, we will receive a sip of living water, of the Spirit of everlasting life. It may conceive within our spirits. With the grace of God it may nourish a seed that has been planted deep within our spirits. If we continue to nourish this seed with the Word of God, it will grow into a fountain of many living waters so that we may share this nourishment of knowledge with others so that they will become fountains that are many living waters. This is the will of God, to live and share His Word in the world.

There are many religions of the world. Religion of any kind cannot fully nourish this seed. An intimate relationship with the Spirit of everlasting life can, and will, if we drink of it daily. To fully understand the Word of God, the Bible, is to fully understand the Words of Jesus. He is the tabernacle of God Himself (Rev. 21:3). In this unique time, known as the church age or the age of grace, we are no longer tied to the laws and rituals of religion. The tabernacle of God Himself has brought us the intimate knowledge of who He is and how we must worship Him, whether we are Jewish or Gentile! To truly worship Him is to live our lives in His Spirit and in the truth of His Word (John 4:24). If we will do this in the Spirit of Christ Jesus, we will understand that there is a difference in, and of, religion and how it can be Satan's philosophy of truth.

I pray that you will understand and not be offended by my Words. I realize many of us at one time or another, or even now, may be devoted to our precious religions! Remember this: so was our great apostle Paul of the New Testament, and he killed Christians! Paul learned to know God intimately, from the Words of Jesus Christ only! This is the same for any of us on this planet to this very day! Whether we are Jewish or Gentile! Whether we are called Christian or non-Christian. We must simply believe in the Words of Jesus, which is the Word of God (John 3:34 KJV).

The first people to be tagged with the name of Christian were residents within the city of Antioch (Acts 11:26 KJV). This name was given to them by the people of that time. If we do not wish to be called Christians–though

I can't imagine why that would be—but we believe the Words of Jesus, we are still children of God and must know Him intimately. How can we come to this intimate knowledge of God? From the Words of Jesus, which is the Word of God—the Holy Bible!

The Bible is not a book of religion of any kind. It is the book of wisdom, knowledge, and truth, as the Word of God. The Word of God is all power and authority. Therefore, it is the wisdom and knowledge of the very existence of the one and true God. If we are so-called Christians, or non-Christians, and we follow our precious religion devotedly but never seek God diligently, our efforts may be in vain. I don't know; I am not God. But if we do not know Him intimately, how can He know us intimately?

This is truly freedom of choice, which He gave us. He knows who we are; He created us. But do we truly know Him in an intimate relationship as our Father in Heaven? Or do we worship Him as an all-powerful God, the creator of all, with no true intimate knowledge of His love for us? Remember God came to His creation as the creation of man (Jesus) for the salvation of His creation (1 Tim. 3:16; Matt. 1:23; John 1:10; Rev. 21:3; John 1:14; Isa. 9:6; John 3:16).

God so loved the world that He came as the Son of God, His creation of the only anointed begotten of the flesh, His earthly vessel, for the salvation of His creation! This is an Almighty, all-loving, all-merciful God with an intimate love for His creation! This is my God, my Father in Heaven. Do we truly know Him as the one and true God?

We must seek God diligently no matter what religion we choose to follow. Remember this: the world is full of religion! We must seek God diligently, whether we are Christian or non-Christian, as the world may label us. To truly know God intimately is not a religion. It is the knowledge and wisdom of His Word, which is His true identity. This is not a religion of any kind but a true and intimate knowledge in a relationship with our Father in Heaven, the creator of all! This intimate knowledge is given to us by the life, the death, the burial, and the resurrection of Jesus, the Christ. It is given to all humankind, Jews or Gentiles, Christian or non-Christian!

Please read and understand the intimate knowledge of God, the Word of God, the Holy Bible!

CHAPTER 1

A Biblical Study for Truth

A S THE TITLE OF THIS book is *Religion: Satan's Philosophy of Truth*, one might ask, what religion am I speaking of? When I say religion, I'm referring to all religions of the world. This would most certainly include all so- called Christian religions as denominations and doctrines, to a certain degree. Why? Satan is a deceiver. He is here to confuse and dismantle the Word of God. He has done so through the many religious teachings in and outside of Christian belief.

This book will focus on the reality of all religions of the world and the deceptions within. Though I may be considered by many to be a religious person, I cannot fully appreciate that statement. It is truly offensive to my spirit and to my understanding of God's Word. I am a biblical man—a child of God! Though I am tagged with the title of Christian, I do not follow any religion. Let me make this clear!

Any dictionary will define *religion* as something like this: Religion is an organized belief system. It will teach a belief of the existence of the world, the universe, and all creation by God or gods.

We can clearly see from all the religions of the world that religion is an organized belief system. This is not to say that a so-called religion is of no use. However, a "one true religion" in the church age or in the age of grace does not exist. A belief system could be of great value if properly understood according to the teachings of God Himself.

A great many people of this world will not seek God for themselves. They will merely rely on a belief system. The knowledge of God and your relationship with Him is your responsibility and yours only. If an organized belief system has this knowledge of God, then many should congregate to it. The church of God (His followers) are not tied to rules, regulations, and laws.

I have sought after the identity of God diligently for more than thirty-five years. I truly believe that the truth of what is called religion lies within the pages of the Holy Bible. I am constantly seeking knowledge about God and about what the many non-Christians of the world believe. I am constantly seeking God and knowledge of what all Christians believe in when it comes to the many so-called religions, or denominations, of Christianity.

Christianity is not a religion; it is a relationship with God. We are flesh, and He is Spirit! We must receive His Spirit! This is why I know all religions of the world, including Christianity, have both truth and error. This is why I know religion can be, and many times is, the philosophy of Satan. If you can say that you love God and wish to serve Him in this life, then be sure of what you serve. Is it God that you serve, or is it your idol, religion?

Though I have diligently sought after God across many religions, I can boldly state that the Holy Bible is the truth about God. Why? Because it is the Word of God, and it is for everyone on the planet, if only they would read it! Seek God diligently! If you say you love and want to serve Him, then truly be certain you know how to serve Him.

As Christians, we believe in one God. This would be God Jehovah, our Father in Heaven. This knowledge is given to us by the teachings of the Old Testament. We also know and believe that His created Son, Jesus Christ, is God. This knowledge is given to us by the New Testament. Christ was God Jehovah in Spirit and fullness, in an anointed flesh vessel known as the Christ. Read Colossians 2:9 and John 3:34 in your Bible.

This truth from the Word of God is also found in Revelation 21:3: "And I heard a loud voice from Heaven saying, 'behold, the tabernacle of God is with men, and He will dwell with them, and they shall be His people. God Himself will be with them and be their God'" (NKJV). This verse, of course, is speaking of Jesus Christ.

In the many belief systems and denominations of Christianity, some may claim their faith as a religion only. What faith are you is a common question. The answer is quickly and most commonly given by the name of a religion or denomination such as Catholic, Baptist, Presbyterian, Lutheran, Pentecostal, Mormon, Jehovah's Witness, Amish, and so on. The truth of this matter, however, is the Word of God. The Holy Bible teaches us that there is one God, one faith, and one baptism. The one God, of course, is Christ. The one faith is Christ because He is our salvation. The one baptism is Christ because we received the gift of His Holy Spirit, a true baptism. This knowledge is given to us in the Old Testament, and it comes to life in the New Testament. Within the many belief systems of so-called Christian religions and denominations, there is much confusion and deception. Why? Satan! He has performed his duty well. He is the author of deception and a liar.

In this unique period of time–known as the church age or age of grace–we are taught by the Word of God to live a life of flesh in His Spirit and in the truth of His Word. This is true worship, to live a life of flesh but as the expression of the Holy Spirit. Christ said in John 20:21–22, "Peace to you! As the Father has sent Me, I also send you. Receive the Holy Spirit" (NKJV). Jesus, the flesh man, a container or vessel for the Almighty Holy Spirit, is expressing with actions and Words His true identity (Col. 2:9; John 3:34). We the people of the church age are taught by Jesus to do the same.

This is not a religion of any kind. This is a true and intimate relationship. Christ has brought us the truth and knowledge of the one and true God. Christ was the Spirit of God in the world in an anointed flesh vessel. We as the church or as the saints of God are the expression of the Spirit of God through the knowledge of Christ. We are not 100 percent the Spirit of God, as Christ, but we are of flesh as Christ was of flesh–an expression of the Holy Spirit in the world today.

This is true worship as children of God with our Father in Heaven. This is not religion. This is a true and intimate relationship. Read these Words of 2 Corinthians 13:5: "Examine yourselves as to whether you are in the faith. Test yourself. Do you not know yourselves, that Jesus Christ is in you? Unless indeed, you are disqualified" (NKJV). This scripture is plainly asking us if we are living in the Spirit of Christ, expressing His Spirit in the world as He did, or if we are living life according to our own earthly spirits. If the latter, then we are merely visiting the church of God on Sunday.

We must not live in the rituals of religious doctrine but in the Spirit of God and in the truth of His Word.

This is not just for Sundays but for every day of our given lives. This truth is found in John 4:24: "God is Spirit, and those who worship Him must worship Him in Spirit and in truth" (NKJV). This scripture is telling us that we must abide in the Spirit of Christ (the Holy Spirit) and in the truth of His Word, which is in the knowledge He taught us. And then we must live it in this life.

The word *religion* is mentioned only five times in the entire Bible. It is first found in Acts 26:5, where it says, "They knew me from the first, if they were willing to testify, that according to the strictest sect of our *religion* I lived a Pharisee" (NKJV, emphasis added). In this scripture, Paul is pleading his case to the king. He is saying that everyone who was present knew that he was brought up in the Jewish religion. He then says that if anyone would testify on his behalf, he or she would bring this knowledge to the king. This is the knowledge that he was a very strict and devoted person in the Jewish religion—not only in the practice of the religion but also in the knowledge of the ancient laws of the Jewish religion. This means Paul lived religiously. This means Paul would live life as pure and clean without spot or blemish. We all know Paul was a man of flesh—a human being.

Now there are many religions throughout the world. There are many Christian and non-Christian religions. We all know that, in any religion, we cannot live without spot or blemish. This, of course, means to have no sin. This is why in the Jewish religion, animal sacrifice was offered to God for the atonement of sin. As we know today, this was all symbolic to the cross of Christ. The earthly tabernacle of God Himself, who lived among men, was offered as the ultimate sacrifice for the redemption of sin—for both Jew and Gentile.

Remember God is Almighty, all-knowing, all-loving, and all-merciful. This world is His creation! We, the people of this world, are His creation! Therefore, the salvation of humankind was the responsibility of God Himself. Read these Words of 1 Timothy 2:3–7:

> For it is good and acceptable in the sight of God our Savior, who desires all men to be saved and come to the knowledge of truth. For there is one God and one mediator between God and men, the man Christ Jesus, who gave Himself a ransom for all, to be testified in due time. For which I was appointed a preacher and an apostle I am speaking the truth in Christ and not lying a preacher of the Gentiles in faith and truth. (NKJV)

According to the scripture above, Paul is proclaiming that he was in the Jewish religion of the Old Testament. But now he is preaching the truth in the Christ of the New Testament as the Word of God. This is not a religion of any kind. This is faith and in truth of the Word of God. Which brings us to the knowledge of the one and true God. This knowledge, as an intimate relationship, is brought to the world by God Himself, God's earthly tabernacle, Jesus Christ.

The second and third time the word *religion* is mentioned in the Bible is in the King James Version, not the New King James Version: "For ye have heard of my conversation in time past in the Jews' *religion*, how that beyond measure I persecuted the church of God, and wasted it: and profited in the Jews' *religion* above many my equals in my own nation, being more exceedingly zealous of the traditions of my fathers" (Gal. 1:13–14, emphasis added).

In these two verses, Paul is claiming the past love and devotion he had for his religion. He is also claiming that he has profited well in the religion and traditions of his forefathers. Paul had lived in a religion of the Old Testament established by God from the bloodline of Abraham, Isaac, and Jacob, all the way down to David. Then from the bloodline of David came the Jewish Messiah, Jesus the Christ. He would be the root and the truth of the Old Testament and the New Testament.

The fourth and fifth time the word *religion* is mentioned in the Bible is in James 1:26–27: "If anyone among you thinks he is religious, and does not bridle his tongue but deceives his own heart, this one's *religion* is useless. Pure and undefiled *religion* before God and the Father is this: to visit orphans and widows in their trouble, and to keep oneself unspotted from the world" (NKJV, emphasis added). By these two verses, I can plainly see that it is not religion of any kind that brings us to salvation. No matter how religious and righteous we feel in our devotion to God by a religion, no one in this world can keep him- or herself unspotted by the sin in this sinful world. We must receive salvation through the knowledge of Jesus the Christ, the tabernacle of God Himself (Rev. 21:3)!

In the Old Testament, the Jewish religion was established by God. It was given to the Jewish people and the Jews only. Even then, there were many religions in the world. These were known as pagan religions. These religions did not have contact with the one and only God of creation, but His chosen people of the Jewish religion did through the prophets who spoke directly with God during that time in history. It was the only knowledge of the one and true God. From that religion established by God came the root of all Christian faith. When Jesus was born, it was also the birth of a new period of time–a New Testament. When Jesus gave up His life for us and died in the world, this was also the death of the Old Testament as a *religion*! The New Testament was born and so was our intimate knowledge and relationship with the Holy Spirit through the life of Christ Jesus, our mediator! Not only for Jews but for everyone in this world!

Within the Christian belief, we have many so-called Christian religions. This would be so-called churches or beliefs as faith. No! We are the church, and our faith is Christ! I just wonder what the unbelieving world must think of us Christians! We all believe in the one and true God. So why do we have so many Christian religions? Why do we have so many different doctrines? Why do we explain our faith in Christ in so many different ways? My answer is the deception of Satan and his philosophy of truth!

An atheist, or an unbeliever in our faith in Christ, might see us all as foolish and confused souls! We claim that we are speaking truth in our religious doctrines. There is great truth, but there is also great error! Look very closely at the words of the apostle Paul, our New Testament disciple of Christ: "Now I plead with you, brethren, by the name of our Lord Jesus Christ, that you all speak the same thing, and that there be no divisions among you, but that you be perfectly joined together in the same mind and in the same judgment" (1 Cor. 1:10 NKJV).

Also look at the words of Paul in 1 Corinthians 1:12–13: "Now I say this, that each of you says, 'I am of Paul,' or 'I am of Apollos,' or 'I am of Cephas,' or 'I am of Christ.' Is Christ divided? Was Paul crucified for you? Or were you baptized in the name of Paul" (NKJV)? This piece of scripture, of course, relates to the many religions that one can be baptized into today.

Yes, it is true in all so-called Christian religions that one is baptized in the name of Jesus or the Father, Son, and Holy Spirit, which is Jesus the Christ. There is no division! The problem is that in the many Christian religions there is division in His Word and how it is taught! Remember John 1:1: the Word was God! Do we truly understand who He is and what He has done for us? This, of course, is in relation to the tabernacle of God Himself (Rev. 21:3)! God is Jesus the Christ, Father, Son, and Holy Spirit, all in one! Read Isaiah 9:6 in your Bible!

It is no great wonder to me why some Muslims would want to kill Christians and Jews! How can I say this? These religious fanatics believe they are devoted to the one and true God as well. How do I know this? I have been reading the Quran. This book of the Muslim faith has much truth but mingles with great error! The problem with some Muslims is the same problem that Paul, our New Testament apostle, had. (Remember the scriptures; Paul killed Christians!) These fanatic and religious Muslims don't know the one and true God's identity!

The identity of God for other Muslims, and many other religious people, may be mistaken as well! Many of us Christians who claim we believe in one God may not truly understand His identity as well. Also, many of us Christians may not truly understand what it is to be a Christian. Why? Religious doctrine! It is truly the philosophy of Satan! How can we as Christians express to the world that we have a solid foundation of truth when our faith itself has so many different religious beliefs?

Look at the words of Paul in 2 Corinthians 10:12: "For we dare not make ourselves of the number, or compare ourselves with some that commend themselves: but they measuring themselves by themselves, and comparing themselves among themselves, or not wise" (KJV). What I believe Paul is saying here is that many of us follow so-called church doctrine, sitting in a so-called church on Sunday and participating in the rituals of religious belief. Or perhaps we sit around a table having what is said to be Bible study but it is nothing more than so-called church doctrine study. Let me explain. If you are a devoted Catholic and go to a Bible study of the Baptist belief, you will notice that the Word of God is taught quite differently. This would be the same for a Baptist visiting a Pentecostal study, a Pentecostal attending a Mormon study, a Mormon going to a Jehovah's Witness study, and so forth. Though they all will disagree with the doctrines and interpretations, they all agree on the top line, which is the bottom line: Christ Jesus our Savior! Christ is the alpha and omega, the beginning and the end, of the Word of God!

In my mind, I can clearly equate the many people of Christian religions, and others, to a faulty marriage. In a faulty marriage, if one spouse does not respect, feel, or understand the love of the other, there is no true intimate love in the relationship. The spouse in fault may live within the written agreement of marriage but holds no intimate feelings of love and respect for that contract. This is not a true relationship as one spirit in life.

One may see marriage (or religion) as an earthly view only. This would be to follow the contract agreement (or water baptism of a religion) as a set of rules. One may never try to fulfill those rules but still believe that the other will always forgive him or her. One may not appreciate or understand the love from the origin of the marriage (or religion). For out of the marriage contract (or religion) came the root of truth in life and the example of true love. Whether we are Jewish or Gentile, Christ Jesus is our salvation and nothing more!

The truth of the love of Jesus came out of the Jewish religion. God had established this by a promise, or a contract or covenant, with the Jewish people of the Old Testament. At that time, they were the only people on the planet who actually knew of the one and true God. From that religion, or root of knowledge, of the one and true God came the tabernacle of God Himself! Read Revelations 21:3; Matthew 1:23; John 1:14; John 3:16; 1 Timothy 3:16; Isaiah 9:6; and John 1:1. Read and understand these scriptures of the Bible, or Word of God. There are many more!

When Jesus was born into the world, He gave us a greater knowledge of the one and only true God. Jesus, the complete or fullness of the Holy Spirit of God, is in an anointed flesh vessel, the only vessel ever to be born into the world or begotten from and of the flesh, the Christ! He literally shows us who the invisible Spirit of God is through His Words and actions! Jesus the Christ did not bring the world a new religion. Jesus brought us the intimate knowledge of love and a true relationship with love for Him in a marriage. This, of course, is being of one Spirit. This is not the rituals of religion but rather an intimate relationship with God as one in a marriage. The marriage of the Lamb of God! In Deuteronomy 32:39,

Jesus is the *He*: "Now see that I, even I, am He, and there is no God besides Me" (NKJV).

Have you ever watched the movie *The Mummy*? If you have, you may remember one of the characters presenting emblems related to various religious beliefs when he encounters a mummy face-to-face. From a chain around his neck, he raises the emblems one by one for the mummy to see. He raises the cross of Christ, the emblem of Buddha, and the Star of David. This man certainly does not know what religion he should put his trust in. He thinks this will be his salvation against the approaching mummy.

At some time in our lives, many of us may have these same feelings concerning our religion and what we should believe. My answer, or opinion, is none. We should put our trust in the Word of God, which is found in one book only, the Holy Bible. The Bible is not a book of religion one must follow. It does teach religion, and none will save us! But out of one religion, with the knowledge of God, came our salvation, Jesus the Christ! The Bible, or Word of God, will give everyone in the world the knowledge of God and what we should believe!

Let me make this clear! Even though I say religion is the philosophy of Satan, I am not suggesting that we forget our religion. What I am saying, and suggesting, is that we seek God diligently. Whether we are Jew or Gentile, Christian or non-Christian, we must seek God diligently! There are many religions and beliefs of God in the world. There is only one truth. Find this truth through a process of elimination with the knowledge of His Word, the Holy Bible.

In the reality of life on earth, there are only three religions of the world that are crucial. These are the

Jewish religion, the Christian religion, and the Muslim religion. Now when I say religion, I cannot exclude the politics that go with it. Politics and religion are what separates many people of the world. Politics and religion together are the cause of every war since the beginning of time. Though politics and religion are necessities in life, if they are truly mishandled or misunderstood, there will be terrible consequences.

If there were no politics and religion, the people of the world could live in peace and share love for one another. This, of course, is not going to happen in the world as we know it. Why? Satan. He is in the world to confuse and cause great deception. This is why I say religion is Satan's philosophy of truth! When Christ returns to His created world, He will govern with His love, and there will be peace and no deception. Christ is truth. Read Isaiah 9:6 in your Bible.

In the Word of God, we can find the knowledge of these three crucial religions. Though the Muslim religion is not specifically stated anywhere in the Word of God, it gives us the root and origin of its people. These people stem from the bloodline of Ishmael, Abraham's firstborn son. Ishmael was the son of Abraham and Hagar, an Egyptian woman. This was not the perfect will of God but rather the will of Sarah, Abraham's wife. Sarah knew of the promise God had made with Abraham. She knew God had promised them a son who would be the father of many nations. Sarah also knew that she could not conceive and was very old, well beyond the age of having this promised son. Sarah told Abraham to take Hagar, Sarah's handmaiden, to have the child. This was not the perfect will of God. If we do not wait on the will of God but move according to our own will in life decisions, God may allow this because He gave us the right of free will. But if our decisions are outside the will and Word of God, there will be great consequences.

Abraham and Sarah were very old. Even so, Abraham was very happy to have Ishmael and raise him as the promised son. I feel that God was not so happy with Abraham and Sarah's decision to have Ishmael. God is of truth, and He will fulfill His promise. Abraham was perhaps one hundred and Sarah perhaps ninety years of age when God fulfilled His promise. This is clearly a miracle and the true will of God, not the illegitimate son, Ishmael, and his mother, Hagar, the Egyptian woman. Isaac, the perfect will of God, was born into the world as the father of many nations.

Here's where the big problem of religion started. From the bloodline of Abraham, Isaac and Jacob, eventually came the Jewish religion–the one and only religion ever established by God. (Remember–Ishmael for many years was part of this knowledge of the one and true God from his father Abraham. Also remember that Judaism, the religion itself, had not yet been fully established). Out of the Jewish religion came the root and the truth of Jesus Christ in all so-called Christian religions. Also from the bloodline of Abraham and Hagar, the Egyptian woman, eventually came the Muslim so-called religion.

The Muslim religion comes from the teachings of the Quran. This book is said to be a divine message revealed by God to Muhammad, a so-called prophet. It claims that over a period of twenty-three years, the angel Gabriel delivered this message. It is said that in AD 610 in the cave of Hira, outside the city of Makkah, the first verse of the Quran was given and commanded by the angel Gabriel for Muhammad to read. I can plainly see by the words of the Quran and the depth of its teaching message that these people wish to establish a one true and only religion. This is not the perfect will of God.

I feel the truth of God's perfect will is misunderstood by all three crucial religions. The Orthodox Jews and the Muslims still wish to live under the law and a religious doctrine established by the God of the Old Testament. These people are blind to the root and the truth of the Old and New Testaments. Many Christians are blind to the root and the truth of the Old and New Testaments as well. How do I know this? There is only one truth in the perfect will of God.

So why do we Christians have so many religious doctrines of truth? I feel it is because we misunderstand the knowledge of the New Testament. We as Christians want to mimic the Jewish and Muslim peoples and hold on to a theory of one true religion. This is why there are so many Christian religions that claim they are of the truth. In my opinion, the New Testament is not about establishing a one true religion. The New Testament is clearly the knowledge of the one and true God so that we all (the people of the world) can have an intimate relationship with Him. He came to His creation as His creation, the man Jesus Christ, for the salvation of His creation. This is truly the knowledge of the Almighty, all-loving, all-merciful God. This intimate love and knowledge expressed by Jesus Christ is not just for so-called Christians. It is for the Jewish and the Muslim religious people and others as well. If they will only seek God diligently! Read the Holy Bible, the Word of God; it is for everyone on this planet!

CHAPTER 2

The Love of Jesus

WE AS CHRISTIANS BRAG ABOUT the love Jesus has for us and sing songs of His love. I wonder, can Jesus brag in all the heavens about the love we as Christians have for Him? Does He sing to His angels of the love we have for Him? Might His song express our love in the way we live for Him, by the way we act or speak in the truth of His Word? Or is He weeping with tears of love, a love to share with us?

Many of us express the love Jesus has for us. But do we as Christians truly express our love for Him? To truly express our love for Him is to live every day in His Spirit and in the truth of His Word.

Jesus said that the greatest gift is love. Jesus said to love our neighbors as we love ourselves. Jesus said to love our enemies. Do we as Christians live with great concern for the souls of others? It should not matter who they are, where they live, or what they believe. To live in the Spirit of Jesus is to live in the Spirit of love. Pray for the souls of others! Witness the truth of His Word and of His love. Every day of our lives we are meant to express with words the love of Jesus, not so much our love for Him but His love for us. Then we literally live our lives as an expression of love for Him.

Jesus expressed His love for us with His life. This is the ultimate expression of love. Yet His statement of love was not complete until He said, "Father, forgive them, for they know not what they do." Then it was complete, and He gave up His Spirit.

Can we as Christians share this kind of love? Yes, we can! Learn to forgive others for what they say or do in sin. This does not mean that we can forgive sin or forget offensive words. That is the will of Christ only. We can through Christ spiritually crucify our flesh. This means deny the earthly spirit of the natural that will hold revenge or hatred in our hearts. This emotional torment, if allowed to grow in us, could eventually destroy us. If we live in the Spirit of Jesus, He will give us His knowledge of forgiveness. This is not to the benefit of the offender! It is a great benefit to the victim! The Word of God teaches us that we must forgive if we expect to be forgiven, whether it be in the past, present, or future. The Word of God also teaches us that we all fall short in righteousness. If we can see the unrighteousness of others only and illuminate it for all to see, then perhaps we have become a greater offender than the one we have persecuted.

As Christians, it is also important that we learn to forgive ourselves through the knowledge of Christ. Once we come to know Christ, we sometimes dwell on our sinful pasts. Satan is always there to remind us. Remember Christ has forgiven and forgotten our pasts.

In 2 Corinthians 12:1–10, the apostle Paul speaks of how Christ changed his life. In verse 7, Paul explains how the Lord exalted him above measure with an abundance of revelations. But he also claims he had a thorn in the flesh. He says this thorn was a messenger of Satan to buffet (or worry) him. Note, the *Webster's New World Dictionary* defines the word *buffet* as a blow or shock or to punch, hit, or thrust about. We must understand that the Hebrew language is very difficult to translate. We also must take into consideration that the word *buffet* used in scripture is an Old English choice. Even so, I can still see the value of the word. For example, if someone told you something strange about someone or something, you might reply, "That did strike me as odd." Or if you received some bad news, you might say, "That hit me hard. I don't think I can ever forget that blow."

In the King James Version, Acts 26:14 states that Saul, or Paul, kicked against the pricks. In the New King James Version, the word *pricks* is translated as *goads*. The *New World Dictionary* defines the word *goad* as "a sharp pointed stick used in driving oxen" and "any driving impulse." With this knowledge, I can clearly see how Paul hit, or gave a hard blow, to the new Christian belief. Paul strongly kicked, or had a strong thrust of movement, against the Christians' knowledge of truth from the impulse, or guiding Words, of Christ. This is why I strongly believe that the thorn in his flesh was the memory of his past and the messenger of Satan to worry him. This would have been Satan's attempt to confuse the glory in the minds and hearts of the saints of God. This is why it reads in 2 Corinthians 12:9, "And he [Jesus] said to me, my grace is sufficient for thee: for my strength is made perfect in weakness" (KJV). We are taught by the Word of God to forgive others. We are also taught through the knowledge of Christ only to forgive ourselves. For Jesus said, "My grace is sufficient for you."

We as Christians must not live our new beginning with thoughts of the past. Yesterday is gone! Tomorrow may not come! We must live our lives for Christ in the new beginning, which is every given day of our lives. We must worship Him in the Spirit of His love and in the truth of His Word. If we as Christians claim the knowledge of

Christ, we must also claim the knowledge of His love, not just by words but also by actions. We Christians must live the love of Jesus. Jesus Christ came to this world not to condemn. He came to show us His love, not just by His Words but by His actions, that all might be saved. We as Christians should follow the example of the love of Jesus. For actions speak louder than words!

CHAPTER 3

Deception in Religious Beliefs

To fully understand deception in religious beliefs, we must first understand the Word of God in the beginning. When God created Adam and Eve, He created them in the perfect will and image of God (Gen. 1:27). Adam and Eve lived in a relationship with God. God did not establish a religion for them to worship Him. For Adam and Eve, true worship of God was to respect His love and concern for them by obeying His Word. In the very beginning of creation, God gave Adam and Eve (the beginning of human life) a choice! This, of course, is the only way a true loving and intimate relationship with God our Father is possible. To live in respect for God is to live in the knowledge of His love for us by His Word.

In the beginning, Adam and Eve lived in the perfect will of God. They knew no sin and lived with a love in relationship for and under the care of God. This is true worship, to live in respect for His Word and to know that He is our provider. God is our Father in Heaven, and His Word is the knowledge of His love. We must always trust in the Word of God. Did Adam and Eve truly understand or realize the truth of that love and what it means to share an intimate relationship with God? I don't think so! Why? The opportunity of choice first had to be given!

In the beginning, Adam and Eve lived in the Garden of Eden. This was a truly heavenly place, a kingdom on earth. God created this place for Adam and Eve as an expression of love for them and His creation of the world. In the beginning, Adam and Eve and the world had no sin. The world was a paradise with the expression of God's love as a heavenly kingdom on earth. This was, and still is, the perfect will of God.

With this reality as a heavenly paradise, a kingdom on earth to continue forever, there had to be a choice. Can we live with love in an intimate relationship with God through the knowledge of His Word? Adam and Eve were given this choice. The Lord God told Adam not to eat from the tree of knowledge, for if he did, he would surely die (Gen. 2:17). This was God's loving Word. Some may look at this and wonder why. The love of God as a parent, our Father in Heaven, may tell us as children of God not to touch the stove. This would be the will and the love of God as His Word. All we should do is obey His Word. God does not have to explain that the stove is hot and we will be burned! God is the all-knowing, all-loving, all-merciful Almighty God. We need to trust in His Word.

Adam and Eve failed to trust in the Word of God when Satan, God's adversary, tempted them. This also had to be the will of God! Adam and Eve had to make the choice to obey or disobey God's Word. This opportunity was given to them when they were tempted by the will of Satan to eat from the tree of knowledge. Satan told Eve that she would not die but be like God and know good and evil (Gen. 3:4–5 NKJV). Now think about this! If Adam and Eve were living under the total care of God and knew no sin, why would they want to eat from the tree of knowledge? Well think! To know good and evil and to be like God, as Satan told them, was the temptation to be in control of their own lives and of their own will.

We in this life, especially as adolescents, think we can be in control of our own lives. How can we be so foolish when God and His Word (or our parents and their word at that time in our lives) is our only salvation? As adolescents, we know nothing of life and have no true knowledge of how to exist in life; we are under the care of our parents. Comparably, without the knowledge of God's Word, we truly know nothing of life, eternal life, or the salvation that God has offered us.

We the people of this world, descendents of Adam and Eve, live under their decision. We are born into the world with a sinful nature because of their disobedience. (Remember: sin leads to death, so at birth, we are already dead. To achieve everlasting life, we must be reborn in the Spirit of Christ Jesus!) Now, just because I say this, don't put your guilt of sin on Adam and Eve. Remember—we all have the freedom from God to make a choice between good and evil. When Adam and Eve disobeyed God and ate from the tree of knowledge, they had to choose, or understand, what was good and what was evil. This was a big problem for Adam and Eve and many of the descendents who followed after them. It is the same for us today, but we have the Word of God, the Holy Bible, to guide us. If we will only read it! They did not have God's verbal Word any longer or the Holy Bible; this is why sin grew rapidly in the world. The Holy Spirit did not dwell within them; they were not the church or saints of God!

God eventually established a true religion with humankind to give back to the world the root, the truth, and the knowledge of His existence. He started this knowledge with a man He called Abraham (Gen. 12:1–4). Eventually from the knowledge God gave Abraham verbally in conversation with Him, and other prophets as well, the Jewish religion came into existence. Abraham's descendents were given by God verbally the instructions to build a tent that would be the tabernacle of God (Exod. 26:1–37). These people, now known as Jews in the religion of Judaism, were of the one and only true religion ever established by God. The purpose of this religion was to bring the knowledge of the one and true God back into the world.

In the Old Testament, the Jewish religion has proof of its very existence as the one and only true religion ever established by God. These documents are everywhere in the Bible! These historical documents claim the truth of creation, the bloodline from Adam and Eve down to the birth of Jesus Christ and many other people pertaining to the Word of God. Many historical documents were written not only by the prophets of God but by other writers of that era as well.

I am frequently asked how we can believe that the Bible is the Word of God when man wrote it. My answer is this: Man will create documents to prove the knowledge he has learned. These written documents of humankind will testify to the truth he has learned or experienced in life. However, I am sorry to say that some historical documents, though written by humankind, may not be of the truth. For that reason, God gave us the prophecy of His Word. The prophecy proves the truth of His Word before it ever becomes a reality in life on this planet.

This is the true reason I know my God is an all-knowing, wise God. He knew that a one and true religion established by Him and historical written documents would not convince the world of His true existence. Why? The world for centuries upon centuries has had many religions and so-called documents of truth. This, of course, is all of Satan and his philosophy of truth so that the world would fall into his deception. But God established His truth with one true religion of the Jewish people. The Old and New Testaments together prove this knowledge through written documents and prophecy.

The New Testament and the birth of Jesus Christ, which came from within the knowledge of the Old Testament, is our truth. Jesus is the root and the truth of the Old Testament and the New Testament. Jesus was the physical body, vessel, or living tabernacle of God, to exist in the world as flesh (Rev. 21:3). This was not to establish another true religion in the New Testament. The New Testament contains the same truth as the knowledge of the Old Testament. Jesus came to fulfill the law, all scriptures, and prophecy. We now cannot have a true religion, only a true relationship with God our Father, as Adam and Eve did before they fell from the will of God.

Jesus Christ came into the world as taught in the New Testament. This is so that we could establish a true relationship with the God of creation and the God of the Old Testament. Remember the scripture of Isaiah 45:5: "I am the Lord, and there is no other; There is no God besides Me. I will gird you [bind you or hold you in correctness of His truth], though you have not known Me" (NKJV). Remember also the scripture of Deuteronomy 32:39: "Now see that I, even I, am He, and there is no God besides Me; I kill and make alive; I wound and I heal; nor is there any who can deliver from My hand" (NKJV). Jesus is the *He* in that scripture!

God wants us, especially in this time of the church age, to know Him even more intimately than Adam and Eve and the Old Testament saints of God knew Him. They knew of God Jehovah and had no thought of any other God. God is Almighty; He needs the help of no other God to exercise His will of judgment. He did use men and women of the Old Testament to destroy many. God commanded Moses to kill those who would not follow Him and gave the second set of commandments Moses brought down from Mount Sinai (Exod. 32:25–29). God knew these people would never come to Him and acknowledge Him as the one and true God. Remember this was religion, not an intimate knowledge of God. The Jews were His chosen people to use and exercise God's will on earth, at His command only.

Today we are under the blood of Christ, or New Testament, that brought us the intimate knowledge of God by His earthly tabernacle, Jesus the Christ. Jesus is the Savior of the world. Jesus is the same God of the Old Testament. The difference in the New Testament is that we received His Spirit as an intimate knowledge of love and a relationship with Him. This now is offered to everyone in the world. God no longer uses us to exercise His earthly judgment. We are no longer Jewish, the only people in the world to know the true existence of God.

In the New Testament, also known as the church age or age of grace, we are offered an intimate relationship with the God of Heaven, creator of all. We are taught by His Word to live in the love of God. We should not emphasize our faith in God through a religion. We should emphasize and live our lives in faith, from the knowledge of His Word. This may not become a reality to us unless we seek Him diligently.

Now that we have an intimate relationship with God, all final judgment is of Christ and Christ only. The knowledge of Christ and the truth of His Spirit now in the world is the knowledge to free us from the bondage of religion. If we live in the Spirit of Christ, we will live in the Spirit of love. Jesus said to love our enemies (Matt. 5:44), to love thy neighbor as thyself (Matt. 22:39), and to love one another (John 13:34). I know love is the greatest gift of all. It is a gift from Jesus, His Holy Spirit.

Many people follow a religion today and believe that they are exercising the will of God. This religion may convince them that they have the right to kill anyone who is a nonbeliever in their faith. Why? Satan's deception in religious beliefs. This is why I truly believe, by the Word of God in all its knowledge, that Jesus came to abolish religion! Jesus, God's Holy Spirit in a flesh vessel, literally came to this world, His creation, to show us His love and His mercy. This would release us from the bondage of religion! How else could we learn to live together in the Spirit of love as a heavenly kingdom on earth?

But also remember God is a just God. He does have a penalty for rejecting Him. Jesus Christ, the tabernacle of God Himself, may tell someone in the time for judgment to depart from Him, for He does not know that person (Matt. 7:23). I believe it is not that God does not know these people. After all, God created them and knew them before the foundation of the world. I believe it is that they did not know Him in the Spirit of His truth, in His Spirit of love (Jesus), and did not bond together with Him as one Spirit.

In the Old Testament, God sometimes showed His power and His judgment to those who opposed Him with the use of His chosen people. I believe God did this to show the world that He is the Almighty God and the knowledge of His existence was given to only

His chosen people of the Jewish religion, which He had established.

In the New Testament, the age of grace, God shows His love! God came to His creation as the earthly tabernacle, Jesus the Christ. This truth is taught in the Old and New Testaments. God showed His power and authority in the Old Testament. In the New Testament, He shows us His love and mercy. He is still the same God of the Old Testament. In the New Testament, He makes Himself known to the world, not just to His chosen people but to everyone in the world! He came as our Savior. He simply does not want any of us to face His judgment. God is a just and righteous Holy God. If He does not pass judgment on those who oppose Him or His Word, how then can He be a just and righteous Holy God?

Through the life of Jesus Christ, He teaches us His love, His statutes, and His will. He wants us to be with Him forever. He always wants us to know that He is the authority, the Almighty God.

We might *say*, of course, that He is the Almighty God. Adam and Eve knew this but disobeyed His Word. How many times in this life on earth have we disobeyed His Word? God is a just but also loving God. He does not want any of us to face His judgment. This is why we are in the age of grace through the knowledge of Jesus Christ. This is not a license to sin but a time to learn. A time to learn of what God Himself did for us through His earthly tabernacle's life and death on the cross. This is an all-loving, all-merciful God. If we come to Him and live for Him in the truth of His Holy Spirit, He will save us through His loving grace. How do I know this? My God is a just and righteous God; He cannot go back on

His Word! He said, "My grace is sufficient for you" (2 Cor. 12:9). Jesus said, "For God did not send His Son into world to condemn the world, but that the world through Him might be saved" (John 3:17). Jesus also said, "I and my Father are one" (John 10:30).

CHAPTER 4

Heads or Tails

THE EXPRESSION "HEADS OR TAILS" quickly relates to gambling. Many Christians know gambling is not the will of God. This activity can, and most likely always will, lead to a loss in your financial gain. For some, it may be just a few dollars that they can afford to lose. But over a period of time for some, gambling can cause a great deal more than the loss of a few dollars. It destroys some people's lives.

For some people, religion is a gamble. What I mean by this statement is that people follow a religion because their immediate families and the ancestors have done so for decades, even centuries. If so, many may trust and follow this family tradition of religion and feel that they will eventually win the big prize. What prize is this? Eternal life, salvation!

If people are following a religion in hopes of being saved (hitting the big jackpot, eternal life), their efforts may be in vain. I don't know for sure; I am not God. But I do know that following religion blindly and not truly understanding its inner most components (the Word of God) is comparable to playing a slot machine. Some religions (or slot machines) are designed to string you along with joy in your heart and then suddenly take you for all you have invested—your time, your money, and your life. You think not? Read some dark history of the many people who followed religion blindly. Read of the people who loved God enough to follow Jim Jones! Or the people who loved God enough to follow David Koresh! Or, centuries back, of the time when the Catholic Pope granted (having no true authority by God to do so) salvation to the crusaders to go out and kill Muslims in the name of Jesus Christ and Christianity! Or, in this very day, of the Muslims who worship Allah and follow a religion thought to be Islam, such as Isis, and believe it is the will of God to kill Christians and Jews or anyone else who are not believers like them.

Hitler and much of his Nazi regime were Catholic, as was 33 percent of Germany during that time. But were they all true Christians? Hitler and his Nazi regime were responsible for the deaths of millions. I can plainly see the definition of religion as one's belief, but that does not make it truth! This truly is religion, Satan's philosophy of truth! This truly is deception in religious beliefs! Throughout the history of religion, there are literally hundreds of documents that prove this deception. This deception is one's personal beliefs. Your beliefs are not relevant to the truth. We must seek God diligently to learn His truth. Jesus the Christ was a witness of the truth. This means that Jesus, the anointed flesh vessel filled with the Holy Spirit of God, showed us His truth. But if we simply follow a religion and feel righteous in our devotion to God simply because our family ancestry has done so for decades or even centuries, then our beliefs may be in vain and irrelevant to the truth!

If you are going to follow a religion (an organized belief system) devotedly, be sure that you understand its innermost components, meaning how this religion teaches the Word of God. To be absolutely and positively correct in your judgment, you must seek God diligently.

Study the Word of God for yourself. Know from the Word of God only if someone is preaching to you truth. Then go to this place of worship and congregate as the church of God on Sunday.

We must remember that Satan is a deceiver. Satan will use truth mingled with lies to deceive God's children. Satan knows that there is no better way to deceive than to pose as an angel of the light. I believe the thought of a religion of any kind today is the will of Satan. I believe Satan tries to mimic God's will of truth through the false doctrines of religion. After all, the origin of truth, Christ Jesus, came to us from the knowledge of the only true religion God ever established.

I believe Christ, God's earthly tabernacle, came to abolish religion. How and why? After the life, death, burial, and resurrection of Jesus Christ, the knowledge of God and our will to worship Him is given to us through His Holy Spirit. If we will accept the truth of His Word, then and only then, can we worship Him in Spirit and in truth. "God is a Spirit: and they that worship him must worship him in Spirit and in truth" (John 4:24 KJV). This is not a religion of any kind. This is a true and intimate relationship with God. This is a bond with the Spirit of God in the truth of His Word.

Look at the Words of Jesus: "Woman, believe Me, the hour is coming when you will neither on this mountain, nor in Jerusalem, worship the Father" (John 4:21 NKJV). The hour, of course, is His death, burial, and resurrection. The significance of the words "this mountain, nor in Jerusalem" is that the woman was of the Gentile nations and Jerusalem is of Judaism. By this we can understand that salvation is for all, Jews and Gentiles. This would also mean that there is no true religion to follow. We must simply follow Christ in His Spirit and in the truth of His Word, the Word of God! Of course the world bonds Christ with Christianity! But do all Christian believers following a religion truly bond in the Spirit of Christ? Please read 2 Corinthians 13:5!

Please, for the love of God (literally), don't gamble with your eternal life. To follow religion and not understand or know its true components is like playing a slot machine. You may pull the handle and spin the wheels of life. You may sit with great excitement, wondering how it will end. You may feel the excitement as a very much expected win, mainly because of the time and money you have invested. But there is no guarantee in a slot machine or in religion. Seek God diligently! You must know the components of your religion. Religion can be, and often is, Satan's philosophy of truth.

CHAPTER 5

God Is the Creator of All. Is This Also Good and Evil?

IRST, THINK DEEPLY OF SCRIPTURE! Please don't start singing songs of blasphemy directed at me because of my words. First, look at the Word of God, Isaiah 45:7: "I form the *light*, and create *darkness*: I make *peace*, and create *evil*. I the Lord do all these things" (KJV). Notice the four Words in this scripture: light, darkness, peace, and evil. They are all opposites.

Pay close attention to these next two scriptures: "For God doth know that in the day ye eat thereof, then your eyes shall be opened, and ye shall be as gods, knowing *good* and *evil*" (Gen. 3:5 KJV) and "For God knows that in the day you eat of it your eyes will be opened, and you will be like God, knowing *good* and *evil*" (Gen. 3:5 NKJV). Please think deeply of what the scriptures are telling us.

Once Adam and Eve ate from the tree of knowledge, thinking they could be like God or gods, they then perhaps thought they would know all things. Then perhaps they thought they would be in control of their own lives. But what happened? They hid themselves with shame and not just because they were naked! They realized that with this new knowledge, they had exposed themselves to sin by their disobedience. I can clearly see it was a freedom of choice.

This is the same for any us to this very day. We also may want to hide ourselves with shame when caught in a lie or sinful deception. If we, like Adam and Eve, think we can have the knowledge of God Himself, we will make the wrong decisions and expose our sin. This is why we need the knowledge of His Word. He is God and the only one to know all things. His Word will give us the ability to make correct decisions in our freedom of choice. There has to be an opposite for the righteous in the sight of God in order for us to become righteous. Remember we must be born again. If there was no *evil*, then how could we choose? Please think deeply of what I'm saying!

I do not believe that God created the *evil* actions of humankind. But the darkness in us is an absence of His light. His light is His Word. If we have an absence in our knowledge of His Word, then we are in darkness. We are born in the world with a sinful nature. This is not to say that we have committed sin by being born. We are simply born of a sinful nature. The earthly, or natural, human spirit is dead to the Spirit of God. We must be reborn, or recreated, spiritually. A person's body, or vessel, is not one's true identity. It is the spirit! The body dies and will rot away; the spirit, our true identity, goes on into eternity somewhere. If your Spirit is in Christ, you will go with Him. If not, well, that's God's decision. Or was it yours? Do we wish to have peace for all eternity or payment of evil in the absence of His light, which of course is darkness!

In this day of grace, the New Testament, we literally have the character, or light, of God, which is known to us through the Holy Bible. The Bible is His Word and His identity. In the Old Testament of the Jewish religion, I firmly believe that these people knew of God and His

Almighty power as the one and only true God. But did they intimately know Him as we do or can know Him today, *by His light?* In reference to the Old Testament, Jesus said in the New Testament: "Ye neither knew me, nor my Father: if ye had known me, ye should have known my Father also" (John 8:19 KJV). I believe this is the difference between having the Holy Spirit fall upon us and having the Holy Spirit of Christ live within us!

Remember Jesus said to receive the Holy Spirit! This, of course, would be the knowledge of God from the knowledge of Christ, the light of the world, God's earthly anointed vessel for the church age. This light, or knowledge, from Christ is an intimate relationship with God our Father in Heaven. The same God Jehovah of the Old Testament! The same Holy Spirit that fell upon, but did not not dwell in, the prophets and saints of the God of the Old Testament.

In the Old Testament of the Jewish religion, God uses His chosen people to show the world the statue of His judgment, in an earthly view only. In the New Testament, we learn of His heavenly love. From the Old and New Testaments, we can surely see the character of the one and only true God. Clearly shown to us by His earthly tabernacle, Jesus the Christ (Rev. 21:3). Jesus is the light and truth in the world!

God created the world. It was a heavenly paradise, peace on earth. Then Satan came, a creation of God. He presented a choice to the world–Adam and Eve. It was the choice of good or evil. Though it truly is one's choice, the lust of evil, which is when actions create the existence of evil, it is solely our choice. God did this by creating Lucifer, an angel of lust and the desire of evil, to give us this choice. Remember–Lucifer is believed to be an anointed angel of an authority of music and songs of worship in the throne room of Heaven.

I firmly believe that Lucifer had to have known the intimate knowledge of God and had to be placed by God as an authority of worship. It is also my belief that Lucifer had to have known good and evil and the peace of God's Spirit. Lucifer also must have known the absence of His light, which is the calamity of darkness. Read Ezekiel 28:12–17 in your Bible. Then read Isaiah 14:12–14. From the scriptures of the Bible, I can clearly see that Lucifer was a beautiful angel created by God with an authority above all others. I firmly believe that because of Lucifer's knowledge, he thought he could overthrow God and be in control of all things. Lucifer failed to realize that God the Almighty Holy Spirit as His Word is all power and authority.

I believe that Lucifer was full of himself with pride and envy. Then when God created the universe, the world, and humankind, Lucifer was filled with jealousy. Think deeply now. Adam and Eve were created in the perfect image of God. They knew no sin, and the world had no sin in its existence. When Lucifer lost his authority in the throne room of Heaven, his will was to destroy the love of God's creation.

Lucifer was allowed to come to God's creation as Satan, God's adversary. With the lack of true knowledge, Satan came to oppose, or to give a choice to, humankind. Satan's ignorance to the Word of God caused him to present a choice of free will to humankind. Do we love the creation or the creator of all? Satan brought the world a false knowledge, a lie. Satan brought the world a will of pride, envy, and jealousy. He also brought a false knowledge of the existence of the world and who is in control of it, humankind, or God! Jesus the Christ, as the tabernacle of God (Rev. 21:3), brought us His Word. Now, through that opposing knowledge, a true love and intimate relationship with God is possible. It is truly free will given to us by God. It is the only way true love could be established in humankind for God.

This is the reason Lucifer tempted Adam and Eve. Lucifer knew that through the weakness of the flesh (moral beings) they would fall to the will of evil. This, of course, meant to disobey God. Lucifer wanted to be in control of all things. So think now: if it is not of God, it is of the devil. God knew all things before the creation of the world. God knew of the fall of Lucifer, now known in the world as Satan or the devil. God use Satan as His adversary. The creation of Lucifer with a God-given will (a decision of choice) came as the existence of Satan. Satan was not destroyed by God at that time. We the children of God, our Father in Heaven, can now freely choose good (peace with God) or evil. With the knowledge of Christ, we can freely choose an intimate relationship with the God of creation, our Father in Heaven. This, of course, is a true love, one established by choice and not by command.

Think about this deeply with scripture in mind. If God knows all things before they ever exist, then He knew His church, those who would come to Him in love of His Spirit (the light and truth in the world, Christ Jesus). This is before the choice ever existed, as in the beginning. God, in His infinity of existence, already knows our choices. God had a plan for each and every one of us before we were created. He gave us life in the physical world; it was free from God. He also gives us a choice with free will to live for Him, in His plan, in His Spirit, and forever with Him. So then, by choice of God's plan, not our own, we the believers in Christ are one Spirit in Christ, which is also one Spirit in the Father, as the Father is Christ.

The first hint of salvation is mentioned in Genesis 3:22. Including the past, no matter how God works out His plan of salvation for the existence of life here on earth, there is salvation. Whether it be Adam and Eve or those who followed after them until the time of Noah, or any other period, we now live in the church age, also known as the age of grace. Our salvation comes from Christ. He is our salvation! He is our tree of life. He will join us in Spirit with Him, the Spirit of our Father in Heaven. Remember the body is nothing but a container; your spirit is your true identity. So was the anointed flesh body of Jesus–the Son of God in all His Glory, the Christ, the Spirit of God, the *light* of the world!

With all this said, think deeply! In all the world there are many religions and religious beliefs. Just because one religion believes something wholeheartedly, does this make it truth? In the entire world, even in the existence of life itself, there is one truth only. One's belief is not relevant to the truth. Seek God and His truth diligently, *His light is true.* Jesus said He was a witness to the truth (John 18:37). Jesus was the tabernacle of God Himself (Rev. 21:3). If we come to know Christ through the Holy Bible, the Word of God, then we have come to know God, the creator of all. If we can say we know Him, then we are in His Holy Spirit, *the light.* Without the light of God, there will be no end to the darkness in the world, or evil. God's light, the witness of truth Jesus the Christ, destroys the darkness and its fear and gives us peace within His light. God is the creator of all!

CHAPTER 6

Created in the Image of God

PLEASE READ THIS CHAPTER WITH an open mind and heart. In my opinion, this is the truth of scripture. This chapter will explain through scripture how we are reborn in the Spirit of God as one. Remember that these are my opinions, so you decide!

To be created in the image of God is to be reborn of His Spirit. We are born into the physical world of a natural or earthly spirit, which is dead to the Spirit of God! We must be reborn! I am not speaking of the physical body, which is of this world. I am speaking of the spirit, which the physical body contains. I could say that I believe, but I must say that I know that your spirit is your true identity. The truth of this statement is not only in the physical realm but also the spiritual realm. Read John 3:3 in your Bible! Think of scripture and life itself in this world as we know it. Jesus was born into the world as a man of flesh, a human being, a creation of the Holy Spirit. His true identity is the Holy Spirit.

To fully understand this, you must go to the Gospel of John, chapter 1. Read verses 1 through 14. You must also read John 4:24, Matthew 1:23, 1 Timothy 3:16, John 3:16, Isaiah 9:6, and Revelation 21:3. Jesus, the man of flesh, was the Christ, who is of the Holy Spirit. In reference to Jesus the man, Christ is His title, which means He is the anointed one who contains the fullness of God's Spirit, the

Holy Spirit, which is His true identity. Read Colossians 2:9 and John 3:34!

In the same manner that the flesh body of Jesus was born into this physical world, we are born of flesh into this physical world. But unlike Christ, we are not the anointed one. Read Luke 1:35: "And the angel answered and said unto her [Mary], The Holy Ghost shall come upon thee, and the power of the Highest shall overshadow thee: therefore also that Holy thing which shall be born of thee shall be called the Son of God" (KJV). Why is this scripture calling the baby Jesus a Holy thing? I can plainly see that it is because the body is nothing but a container for the spirit, which is one's true identity.

Jesus was an earthly vessel, or container, created by the Holy Spirit to be the Holy Spirit in this physical world. This is why He shall be called the Son of God. God the Holy Spirit came to His creation as His creation—man—to be the salvation of His creation. Jesus was the Spirit of God sent, or created, to be born into the natural physical world (of course, having no sin)! This is why 1 Timothy 3:16 reads, "God was manifested in the flesh" (NKJV). We are all born of the natural, meaning a spirit of this world. We must be reborn, or recreated, in the image of God.

To understand the truth of this, go back to Genesis 3:22. If you will notice, within the second line of that scripture are the words, "And now." These two words are in conjunction with the fall of Adam and Eve and their offspring thereafter. Remember Adam and Eve were created in the perfect image of God; they knew no sin. The world they lived in was a heavenly kingdom on earth. This was and still is the perfect will of God. When Adam and Eve disobeyed God, sin came into the world. They and the world were no longer in the perfect image of God.

Because of Satan, or sin, they were deceived into thinking they could be in charge of their own lives. To be in charge? Yes! To be correct in their decisions? No! We are the descendents of Adam and Eve. We are in charge of our own lives. Take a good look at the world and its existence since the time of Adam and Eve and their fall from the will of God, starting with the death of Abel. Remember Cain and Abel in the book of Genesis. Then remember the history of the world since that time. There have been countless wars and even greater bloodshed since that time. The world has become a killing field because of our decisions.

To be created in the image of God now means for us to be recreated, or reborn, in His Spirit. Remember Satan is a deceiver; he will come in the form of light, but he is of darkness. In darkness there is much confusion because we cannot see things clearly. Jesus is the light; therefore, through the Spirit of God, we will see things clearly.

Because of many religious beliefs and Satan, an impostor of the light within them all, there is great confusion and disagreement in this world. Look closely at the history of the world, of the horrors this has caused through the centuries of our existence. Look closely at the image of humankind without the image of God dwelling within. Humankind will fulfill by choice its lusty desires. Throughout the history of humankind, in this physical world and with the natural spirit of this world, we could eventually destroy ourselves. This is the will of Satan!

God, as Jesus the Christ, His Son, in all His Glory has come to His world as our redeemer! And through the life of Jesus Christ, He is also our mediator. This means that from the knowledge of Jesus Christ, the Holy Spirit, we can become recreated, or reborn, in the Spirit and likeness of God. Without the life of Jesus Christ, our redeemer, how can this sinful world (because of the existence of our sin) ever change or be saved from the will of Satan? Christ is our redeemer, He is our Savior! Without the life of Jesus Christ as our mediator, how could we have ever learned this knowledge of salvation?

Please read the following scriptures in your Bible: Jesus our redeemer (Luke 1:68; Gal. 3:13; Rev. 5:9); Jesus our mediator (Gal. 3:19–20; 1 Tim. 2:5–6; Heb. 8:6; Heb. 9:15; Heb. 12:24), Jesus our salvation (1 Chron. 16:23; 1 Chron. 16:35; 2 Chron. 20:17; Ps. 3:8; Isa. 43:11; Luke 1:47; John 4:42; Acts 5:30–31; 1 Tim. 1:1; 1 Tim. 4:10; 2 Tim 1:10). God is the same yesterday (Old Testament) and today (New Testament). He is a never-changing God.

God did give us a choice of free will. It is now up to us to use this choice in the physical being, as of the natural spirit, and *give it back to God!* This is what it means to give your lives to Christ! We must surrender to Christ! By doing so, we must live in the Spirit of Christ, which is the Spirit of God, the Holy Spirit. We are now reborn as an expression of the Holy Spirit in the world today. Now, and only now, can we see things clearly through the darkness of this world, with the light of the Holy Spirit, and make the correct decisions. This is why John 4:24 states, "God is a Spirit: and those that worship him must worship him in Spirit and in truth" (KJV).

To fully understand this is to become an adopted child of God from this physical world. What I mean by this is that your earthly spirit of the natural is changed, reborn, in the image of Christ. Realize what the scriptures are teaching us. We are one Spirit in Christ, as Christ is one Spirit in the Father. Remember–the Spirit of the Father was in Christ Jesus, the anointed earthly vessel.

Then realize that if we are one in Christ as Christ is one in the Father, it is the Holy Spirit we contain in our earthly vessels, our bodies. But only if we are in Christ Jesus! Though our earthly bodies may die and rot away, our Spirit will live forever in a new spiritual body. The scriptures teach us that God will not put new wine in an old vessel (Matt.9:43. This plainly tells me that our spirit is our true identity, just as Jesus Christ in this physical world, as physical being, was in His true identity, the Holy Spirit, God, our Father of Heaven (Isa. 9:6).

Remember God knew all things before the foundation of the world. God has always known the end results of His creations. We might ask, but if God loves us so very much, why is there so much sickness, despair, hatred, killings, and just plain lack of respect for Him? The answer, of course, is Satan, as sin in the world. We also might ask, if He knew this, then why did He create the world and us to inhabit it in the first place? The answer is because of His Glory. We might say, what glory? We might say the world today is full of hatred and killings because of what one believes, because of Him. If we truly believe this, then we are in darkness.

The glory of God is truly in His light. Those who come to Him in the truth of His Word will shine in His glory. This, of course, is the end result of His creation as we know it today. The world is a beautiful expression of the love and the glory of God. In the beginning of God's creation, Adam and Eve knew of this glory of God. But a choice first had to be made to live in the glory of God forever. This means knowing that He is the Almighty, all-loving God, no questions asked. We will simply live in His glory, as His glory, in the creation of all His glory.

He has called each and every one of us in this world. He has truly yelled at the top of His lungs for the past two thousand years. This, of course, is the church age, the age of grace. He has yelled with His lungs the breath of life that we must receive. That breath of life is the Holy Spirit of the earthly tabernacle, Jesus the Christ, the Spirit of God! If we answer and come to His Spirit, we will become one Spirit in Christ, as Christ is the one Spirit of God, the Holy Spirit! This is the glory of God. We are now created in the image of God! We are not at this time perfect, having no sin. But the blood of Christ will cover our sin. Therefore, the Almighty Holy Spirit will see us in this world as flesh, as the perfect flesh body of Christ. For in the body of Christ, there are many members, no matter how great or small. This simply means that no matter what our status in this life or our knowledge of His Word, we are of the body of Christ. Read chapter 12 of 1 Corinthians. We are the hidden mystery of scripture, the glory of His church, forever with the glory of God, Jesus Christ!

This all, of course, is my opinion. We as Christians should know that faith comes by hearing, and hearing comes from the Word of God (Rom. 10:17). We all should realize that the Word of God, the Bible, is strictly for the mystery of the church. Read 1 Corinthians 2:7–8. The church can be anyone in the world who will read it, believe it, and then live it. This has been no mystery for the past two thousand years. Think about this: never before the cross, and perhaps after His return, will there be a church age or age of grace ever again. We live in a very unique era.

The Old Testament saints knew nothing of the church age or age of grace. They knew nothing of the Holy

Spirit dwelling within them. They knew nothing of the revelations of Christ given to the apostle Paul. We as the church, the saints of God, the bride of Christ, as one body have preached the Word of God for the past two thousand years. Jesus said, "As my Father has sent me, I send you" and "Receive the Holy Spirit" (John 20:21–22 NKJV). Please read the Gospel of John, chapter 17. Pay close attention to verse 21. It is my understanding that Jesus is speaking of His disciples and others who have knowledge of His church. It wasn't until after His death, burial, and resurrection that we could receive His Holy Spirit within us. It wasn't until after the apostle Paul had received revelation from Christ that the ministry of the church was known in the world. But for God our Father in Heaven, it was known before the foundation of the world.

Jesus said, "Greater things shall we as the church do." Jesus said, "He must go to the Father." Read John 14:12. We as the church, the saints of God, are the expression of the Holy Spirit in the world today!

Humankind as a whole is blind to the Word of God. Why? The fall of Adam and Eve in the beginning. Since that time, humankind has been dead to the knowledge and Spirit of God (with the exception of the Jewish people in the established religion of the Old Testament). It is now the church age and the responsibility of the saints of God to plant the seed of life, preach the Word of God, and bring each other to the knowledge and Spirit of God. Let us, the Father, the Son, and the church–as one–make man in our image. Remember–all things were known and complete with God before the foundation of the world. God is the all-knowing Almighty God. His prophecy in the Word of God proves the end result in all things. This is how by faith we know and will believe that His Word is true! We, as the Christian church, are in the family of God! Let us as one body in the Spirit of Christ, in the Spirit of God, work to bring, to lead, to teach, and to preach God's Word to a fallen world! God will use humankind, His creation, to do all things in this world, of His Spirit. Even to write His precious Word, the Holy Bible.

There are three that bear witness in Heaven (1 John 5:1–20). This refers to the Father, the Son, and the Holy Spirit. Remember–we as the church are one in Christ, as Christ is one in the Father. We must realize that the Almighty invisible Holy Spirit is a witness to Himself by His Word. We must realize that Jesus the flesh man in this physical world was a witness of His truth, the Word of God. We must realize that we the church, the saints of God, are also flesh and a witness of His truth as an expression of the Holy Spirit in the world today.

Remember we are one in the Spirit of God. Remember God knows all things and knew the end result of all things before the foundation of the world. In the completion of all things, we as the church will be His glory, as His glory, for His glory, as it was in the beginning with Adam and Eve!

"God so loved the world that He gave His only begotten son, that whoever believes in Him should not perish but have everlasting life" (John 3:16 NKJV). This is the glory of God!

CHAPTER 7

The Fruits It Will Bear

IN THIS DAY AND AGE 2016, I can see the troubles of the world. It is truly a lack of knowledge, or none at all, of the identity of God and the truth of His Word. We are so far away from the true knowledge of God, yet many of us will not seek Him diligently! We simply follow the leaders of our precious religions. I state this boldly and with authority in the knowledge of the Word of God!

Let me say this: I am a Christian first and an American second. I was born in America not by choice but by the will of God. I thank my God to be an American. Though I am so proud to be an American, I do feel in my spirit the shame of America today! Though I feel in my spirit that America is a voice of God, the country has been silenced by the darkness of political correctness. United we stand, and separate we fall. Wake up, America! We are a Christian nation!

Today America is clearly divided. Why has this happened? America has fallen to the lust of sin. You think not? Turn on your television, sit back, and relax as you view the horrors of sin flash before your eyes. We in America today have taken sin so lightly. We must repent like King David of the Old Testament to be the glory of God once more. Through His foreknowledge, God placed us here as a light in a dark world. Look at the history of America; it was not a pretty picture at her birth. But she is glorious in her statutes. You think not? Read our great

American Constitution in its entirety while you still can. God had a plan for this great nation of America. It is up to us to follow through!

In our past, we as Americans abused our great Constitution regarding civil rights. Thanks to a great man of the one and true God, Martin Luther King Jr., a Christian man, his light is still shining brightly. Why do so many of us today still wish to live back in the darkness? We live in a time of new beginning in America. Even so, we cannot destroy the history of America, our past. We should not destroy the monuments of our past. I did say past! It is over! Realize now that we must learn from our mistakes. The nation of America as a body of people is no different. We live in a country of freedom–a freedom of choice and of belief. The problem is that we don't know what we believe. We as a body of people do not know whom we worship! We must seek God diligently! We must teach our past. We must teach God's Word in our schools. Then we will live peacefully in our new beginning. None of us are perfect. We all have the lust of sin planted in our hearts. This is why I know our great Constitution was given by God to our forefathers. It reads, "justice and liberty for all!" That means for people not only here in America for all people, around the globe! America is a voice of God! Wake up, America, before we lose our voice!

America is not the only troubled nation. Every nation on this planet is troubled in one way or another. I should not have to explain the troubles of the world. Watch the news. Listen to what is said in politics around the globe. Witness the fruits that are bearing because of the lack of knowledge in God's Word. You think it is politics. Yes, it is. But it is also religion and the lack of knowledge of the one and true God. I truly believe that America is the greatest nation God has ever planned to exist in this world as we know it. We are a people from around the globe. Many of our ancestors, as well as people today, have come here in hopes of finding a paradise, a kingdom on earth, a place of milk and honey. A better life! This is the truth of America.

But are many coming here today to *be* Americans? Or are they coming to change America? We should not, even as a Christian nation, freely open our borders. We have laws and formalities for legally entering this country. If we continue to let thousands upon thousands of illegal immigrants enter this country, it will break the backbone of America. I should mention that it is a slap in the face to our ancestors and the people who come here today legally. I should also say that by illegally opening our borders, we are in contradiction to our laws. To hastily allow illegal immigrants from around this troubled globe to enter America without exercising the formalities of our law is of great danger to the security of our nation. Satan is making a great move to destroy this country. He has infected her with an illness and now hopes that she will die.

The reality of terrorism around the globe is the reality of the lack of knowledge of the one and true God! Terrorism, whether it comes from a foreign land or it is homegrown here in this great nation of America, is the lack of knowledge of the one and true God, which is the lack of knowledge of His Word. If we live without this knowledge, Satan will convince us of his philosophy of truth. We will then live with the fruits it bears.

Terrorism has been in the world since the fall of Adam and Eve. The *Webster's New World Dictionary* defines the word *terror* as intense fear, something that causes intense fear, the quality of causing such fear, or one who is very annoying or unmanageable. It also defines the word *terrorism* as the use of force or threats to intimidate, for example through political policy, and the word *terrorize* as meaning to terrify, to coerce, to submit, and so forth, by filling with terror.

We the people of this generation are experiencing the fear of terror by those who will terrorize. These people are known as terrorists. Terrorism is an act of Satan because of a person's lack of knowledge. To be the victim of terrorism is also a lack of knowledge. If we the people of this world would seek God diligently and live by His commandments and His statues, we would not experience this horror.

Read chapter 26 in the book of Leviticus. There are many more passages; this is just a sample of what I'm thinking:

> You shall not make idols for yourselves; neither a carved image nor a scared pillar shall you rear up for yourselves; nor shall you set up an engraved stone in your land, to bow down to it; for I am the Lord your God. You shall keep My Sabbaths and reference My sanctuary; I am the Lord. If you walk in My statues and keep My commandments, and perform them. (Lev. 26:1–3 NKJV)

> But if you do not obey Me, and do not observe all these commandments, and if you despise My statues, or if your soul

abhors [to detest, reject, or fail] My judgments, so that you do not perform all My commandments, but break My covenant, I also will do this to you: I will even appoint terror over you, wasting disease and fever which shall consume the eyes and cause sorrow of heart. And you shall sow your seed in vain, for your enemies shall eat it. I will set My face against you, and you shall be defeated by your enemies. Those who hate you shall reign over you, and you shall flee when no one pursues you. (Lev. 26:14–17 NKJV)

This is Old Testament scripture and pertains to the Jewish people of the Old Testament. They were God's chosen people in that period of time. In this era of the New Testament, we the people of this world are all His people, and His knowledge has been given to us. It is the Holy Bible, the Word of God. He is the same God of the Old Testament and the New Testament. His commandments and His statues are the same today. God is a never-changing God! He may turn His face or His back to those who will not honor Him as their God. But His true judgment is at the end of life as we know it.

To follow a religion of any kind but never seek God diligently may produce a tree of deadly fruit. Religion can be, and often is, Satan's philosophy of truth.

Printed in the United States
By Bookmasters